Spreadsheets Are Killing Your Business

AND WHAT YOU CAN DO ABOUT IT

Dan Golding

A2 Solutions Limited

Copyright © 2024 by Dan Golding.

All rights reserved. No part of this publication may be reproduced, distributed or transmitted in any form or by any means, including photocopying, recording, or other electronic or mechanical methods, without the prior written permission of the publisher, except in the case of brief quotations embodied in critical reviews and certain other noncommercial uses permitted by copyright law. For permission requests, write to the publisher, addressed "Attention: Permissions Coordinator," at the address below.

Dan Golding
A2 Solutions Limited
www.A2Solutions.co.uk

Contents

Introduction 6

The Spreadsheet Trap 13

    Business Risks Using Spreadsheets 16

The Advantages Of A CRM 23

    Understanding CRMs 23

    Different Types Of CRM 27

    Factors to Consider When Choosing CRM Software 30

Other Off-The-Shelf Solutions 33

    Benefits Of Integrating Off-The-Shelf Software Into Your Workflow 39

Bespoke Software Solutions 44

    Understanding The Risks Of Bespoke Software .. 48

Working Out What Your Business Needs 53

Documenting Current/Desired Processes 58

Choosing The Right Vendor 63

Managing The Project 68

Types Of Project Management Methodologies ..69

The Project Manager Within Your Company 73

Implementing The New System 77

Overcoming Resistance To Change 86

Strategies For Overcoming Employee Resistance 91

Maximizing The Benefits 96

Looking Ahead...101

Trends in Software Development......................102

Strategies for Continuous Improvement through Technology Adoption 104

Final Thoughts 107

Dedicated to my truly amazing team of technical wizards and the past, present and future clients that I have had the pleasure to work with.

The advance of technology is based on making it fit in so that you don't really even notice it, so it's part of everyday life.

—Bill Gates, Co-Founder of Microsoft

CHAPTER 1

Introduction

In today's fast-paced and ever-evolving business landscape, adaptability and efficiency are no longer just desirable traits but essential components for success. As the digital revolution continues to transform industries across the globe, businesses of all sizes face the pressing need to embrace technology to remain competitive and sustainable. Among the myriad of technological advancements, software solutions stand out as powerful tools capable of streamlining operations, enhancing productivity, and driving growth.

This book is a comprehensive guide for business owners and entrepreneurs navigating the complexities of implementing software, Customer Relationship Management (CRM) systems, and other off-the-shelf solutions into their organizations. It explores the fundamental shifts occurring in business management paradigms and underscores the critical importance of moving beyond reliance on traditional spreadsheets towards more sophisticated and integrated software platforms.

Gone are the days when spreadsheets were the default go-to solution for managing data and processes within businesses. While spreadsheets served their purpose in the past, they have become increasingly inadequate for the demands of modern enterprises. As businesses scale and complexities grow, the limitations of spreadsheets become painfully evident, leading to inefficiencies, errors, and missed opportunities.

The proliferation of off-the-shelf software and systems presents a transformative opportunity for businesses to revolutionize their operations. From Enterprise Resource Planning (ERP) systems to specialized CRM platforms and project management tools, there exists a vast ecosystem of software solutions tailored to address the unique needs of different industries and business functions.

However, despite the clear advantages that software solutions offer, many businesses remain hesitant to adopt them. This hesitation often stems from a combination of factors, including concerns about cost, implementation challenges, and apprehension about disrupting existing workflows. This book aims to demystify the process of selecting, implementing, and optimizing software solutions, empowering business owners to embrace technology as a catalyst for growth and innovation.

Through practical insights, real-world case studies, and actionable strategies, this book will equip readers with the knowledge and tools they need to navigate the complexities of software implementation successfully. From defining business requirements and evaluating vendor options to managing change and maximizing return on investment, each chapter provides invaluable guidance to help businesses leverage software solutions effectively.

In the following chapters, we will delve into the various aspects of software implementation, addressing common challenges, best practices, and emerging trends in the ever-evolving landscape of business technology. Whether you're a small business looking to streamline operations or a large enterprise seeking to stay ahead of the curve, this book will serve as your indispensable companion on the journey to modernizing your business.

It's time to embrace the future of business management. Let's embark on this transformative journey together and unlock the full potential of your organization through the power of software solutions.

Testimonial From Tom Gormanly Former CEO, Safe Hands Plans Limited

In early 2020, I stepped into the role of CEO at Safe Hands Plans Limited, a company that had recently been acquired by a private equity firm. My primary objectives were to grow sales and prepare the business for FCA regulation.

However, it quickly became clear that the business was in disarray, lacking proper systems and controls. Growth had to be put on hold until we could establish a solid structure. The business was managing millions of pounds under trust and collecting substantial monthly payments through various channels, yet there was no clear way to reconcile these funds to individual customers. The existing CRM was devoid of financial data, and staff usage was hindered by the absence of structured systems, controls, or procedures. The business was essentially running on a tangled web of unstructured and uncontrolled spreadsheets.

Recognising the urgency of the situation, I decided we needed to completely rebuild the CRM to incorporate financial data, which required both a systems developer and a systems analyst. Dan Golding and his team were selected for this critical task. Dan spent two weeks in our office, meticulously documenting every process and interaction to understand our operations fully.

Within my first 90 days, thanks to Dan and his team, we had a detailed and documented plan to reconcile the business, implement systems, procedures, and controls, and establish a platform for growth and regulatory compliance. The new system reduced case processing time from 10 working days to one day and provided a 100% clear view of new customer financial reconciliation. Within two years, we were on track to reconcile approximately 3.5 million historical financial transactions.

Having all our data centralised enabled us to profile our ideal customer accurately, allowing for precise targeting of new prospects and significantly better returns on our marketing spend. This investment, though substantial, proved to be the best Safe Hands Plans had ever made. It was transformational, and the credit goes entirely to Dan Golding and his exceptional team.

Postscript: Due to irregular financial dealings outside the scope of Safe Hands Plans Limited, which were beyond our control, the company unfortunately did not complete its journey to FCA regulation. Nevertheless, the positive impact of Dan Golding and his team's work remains indisputable.

Testimonial From Michelle Kemp COO, MyDigiSafe Limited

MyDigiSafe started out as an idea in 2016, intended as a 'give-away' for customers of a specific estate planning business. It was designed to be a personal digital data storage service aimed at simplifying succession planning and incorporating a 'member-get-member' feature to expand its reach, along with generating subscriber income through its premium service. The platform was built, tested, and ready for launch in 2017. Unfortunately, the firm it was designed to support ceased trading later that year, halting MyDigiSafe's formal launch and necessitating a new route to market.

In 2018, MyDigiSafe began operating as a standalone business. However, without the anticipated customer influx from the initial estate planning firm, growth was slow and modest. In 2023, we decided to re-evaluate the platform's purpose, aims, and objectives, which led us to engage Dan Golding and his team.

Dan quickly identified that while several personal digital data storage services existed, none had sufficiently defined their purpose to achieve significant market traction. Together, we determined that MyDigiSafe needed to differentiate itself clearly. Dan suggested that to truly make succession planning easier, MyDigiSafe should integrate seamlessly with the

Probate-Toolkit, another innovative project on which he was working.

Dan and his team have completely rebuilt MyDigiSafe from the ground up, employing the latest coding techniques and security measures. The revamped platform not only continues to provide valuable personal data storage to support users, their attorneys, and executors but also integrates directly with the Probate-Toolkit. This integration facilitates DIY probate applications and supports professional intervention when needed.

The collaboration between MyDigiSafe and the Probate-Toolkit is set to revolutionise the estate planning sector. This transformative development is the result of a collective effort, with Dan and his team bringing their technical expertise and vision, and our team providing strategic insights and support.

Together, we have breathed new life into MyDigiSafe, positioning it for substantial impact and success.

CHAPTER 2

The Spreadsheet Trap

In the digital age, spreadsheets have long served as the backbone of countless business operations. From financial analysis to inventory tracking, these versatile tools have been relied upon for their simplicity and flexibility. However, as businesses evolve and grow in complexity, the inherent limitations of spreadsheets become increasingly apparent, often hindering rather than facilitating efficient operations. In this chapter, we'll explore the various constraints and challenges associated with spreadsheet dependency and highlight the need for businesses to embrace more robust and integrated software solutions.

Data Fragmentation and Duplication

Spreadsheets are notorious for leading to data fragmentation and duplication within organizations. With multiple versions of the same spreadsheet circulating among employees, inconsistencies and inaccuracies are bound to arise. This fragmentation not only undermines data integrity but also complicates collaboration and decision-making processes.

Limited Scalability

While spreadsheets may suffice for small-scale operations, they quickly become unwieldy and inefficient as businesses grow. Managing large volumes of data across numerous spreadsheets becomes a daunting task, often resulting in performance issues and sluggish response times. Additionally, the manual effort required to maintain and update spreadsheets becomes increasingly unsustainable as workload increases.

Lack of Automation

One of the most significant drawbacks of spreadsheets is their limited capacity for automation. While basic formulas and macros can automate certain tasks, they pale in comparison to the sophisticated automation capabilities offered by dedicated software solutions. Without automation, businesses are forced to rely on manual data entry and manipulation, leading to errors, inefficiencies, and wasted time.

Security Concerns

Spreadsheets are inherently vulnerable to security breaches and data leaks, especially when shared via email or stored on unsecured servers. With sensitive business information often scattered across multiple spreadsheets, the risk of unauthorized access and data theft is heightened. Moreover, the lack of audit trails and access controls makes it challenging to track changes and maintain data confidentiality.

Limited Analytical Capabilities

While spreadsheets excel at basic calculations and data manipulation, they fall short when it comes to advanced analytical tasks. Complex data analysis, predictive modelling, and scenario planning are beyond the capabilities of most spreadsheet software. As a result, businesses miss out on valuable insights and opportunities for strategic decision-making.

Dependency on Manual Processes

Perhaps the most significant limitation of spreadsheet dependency is the reliance on manual processes. From data entry to report generation, much of the work is performed manually, leaving ample room for human error and inefficiency. This manual dependency not only increases the likelihood of errors but also stifles productivity and innovation within the organization.

In conclusion, while spreadsheets have served as a staple tool for businesses for decades, their inherent limitations make them ill-suited for the demands of modern business operations. To thrive in today's competitive landscape, businesses must recognize the shortcomings of spreadsheet dependency and embrace more advanced and integrated software solutions. In the following chapters, we'll explore the benefits of transitioning from spreadsheets to dedicated software platforms and provide practical guidance for successful implementation and adoption.

Business Risks Using Spreadsheets

The Perils of Spreadsheet Errors

1. **Human Error:** Spreadsheets are prone to human error, whether it's a typo in a formula or a misplaced decimal point. Such mistakes can have far-reaching consequences, leading to inaccurate financial

forecasts, faulty analyses, and misguided business decisions.

2. **Version Control Issues:** Collaborative spreadsheet work often leads to version control challenges. Without proper tracking mechanisms in place, users may inadvertently work on outdated versions of a spreadsheet, leading to confusion and inconsistencies in data.

3. **Complex Formulas:** Complex formulas increase the likelihood of errors. Even seasoned spreadsheet users can struggle with intricate calculations, especially when dealing with large datasets or nested functions.

Data Loss and Integrity Concerns

1. **File Corruption:** Spreadsheets stored on local devices are susceptible to file corruption, which can result from hardware malfunctions, software crashes, or viruses. Without proper backup measures, organizations risk losing critical data.

2. **Accidental Deletion:** Human error can also lead to data loss through accidental deletion of files or important spreadsheet cells. Without a robust data recovery strategy, retrieving lost information can be a daunting task.

3. **Lack of Data Governance:** In the absence of proper data governance protocols, spreadsheets can become breeding grounds for data inconsistency and inaccuracy. Without standardized formats and validation rules, the integrity of the data may be compromised.

Security Vulnerabilities

1. **Unauthorized Access:** Spreadsheets stored on shared drives or cloud platforms may be vulnerable to unauthorized access. Weak password protection and lax security measures can expose sensitive business data to malicious actors.

2. **Data Breaches:** A single breach in spreadsheet security can have devastating consequences, leading to financial losses, reputational damage, and legal repercussions. Hackers may exploit vulnerabilities in spreadsheet software or intercept data during transmission.

3. **Compliance Risks:** Organizations operating in regulated industries face additional compliance risks associated with spreadsheet security. Failure to

protect sensitive data can result in non-compliance with regulations such as GDPR, HIPAA, or SOX.

Mitigating Risks and Best Practices

1. **Invest in Training:** Provide comprehensive training to employees on spreadsheet best practices, including formula auditing, version control, and data validation.

2. **Implement Automation:** Leverage automation tools to reduce manual errors and streamline spreadsheet processes. Automated data validation and error-checking routines can help detect anomalies and inconsistencies.

3. **Utilize Collaboration Tools:** Implement collaboration tools that allow real-time editing and version tracking to ensure seamless collaboration among team members.

4. **Establish Backup Protocols:** Regularly back up spreadsheet files to secure locations, both onsite and offsite, to mitigate the risk of data loss due to file corruption or accidental deletion.

5. **Enhance Security Measures:** Implement robust security measures, such as encryption, access controls, and multi-factor authentication, to safeguard

spreadsheet data against unauthorized access and cyber threats.

Embracing Efficiency

As we've already seen, spreadsheets (while useful) do have their inherent limitations, whereas a true software solution offers the following advantages:

Streamlined Workflows

Software solutions are purpose-built to streamline workflows and automate repetitive tasks. By integrating disparate processes into a unified platform, businesses can optimize efficiency and minimize manual intervention.

Scalability and Flexibility

Unlike spreadsheets, software solutions are designed to scale with the evolving needs of businesses. Whether it's accommodating growing data volumes or adapting to changing requirements, scalable software platforms offer unmatched flexibility.

Enhanced Collaboration

Collaboration is seamless with software solutions that enable real-time communication, shared access to data, and collaborative editing features. Teams can collaborate more effectively, irrespective of geographical locations or time zones.

Advanced Analytics

Software solutions empower businesses with advanced analytics capabilities, including predictive modelling, machine learning, and business intelligence tools. These insights enable data-driven decision-making and provide a competitive edge in the market.

Security and Compliance

Robust security features and compliance controls are integral to modern software solutions, ensuring the confidentiality, integrity, and availability of data. Encryption, access controls, and audit trails safeguard sensitive information from unauthorized access and data breaches.

CHAPTER 3

The Advantages Of A CRM

Maintaining strong relationships with customers is paramount to success. Customer Relationship Management (CRM) has emerged as a powerful strategy and technology solution to help businesses effectively manage interactions with their customers. In this chapter, we will delve into what CRM entails and explore the myriad ways it can benefit businesses of all sizes and industries.

Understanding CRMs

Customer Relationship Management, or CRM, is a comprehensive approach to managing interactions and relationships with current and potential customers. At its core,

CRM involves leveraging technology to organize, automate, and synchronize sales, marketing, customer service, and support activities.

CRM software serves as the central hub for storing and managing customer information, such as contact details, purchase history, communication preferences, and interactions across various channels. By consolidating this data in one place, businesses gain valuable insights into customer behaviour, preferences, and needs, enabling them to deliver personalized experiences and build long-lasting relationships.

Key Components of CRM

1. **Contact Management:** CRM software allows businesses to capture and store detailed information about leads, prospects, and existing customers. This includes demographic data, communication history, and interaction logs, providing a holistic view of each customer's journey.

2. **Sales Automation:** CRM streamlines the sales process by automating repetitive tasks such as lead scoring, opportunity management, and quote generation. Sales teams can prioritize leads, track deal progress, and forecast revenue more accurately, leading to increased efficiency and productivity.

3. **Marketing Automation:** CRM enables targeted marketing campaigns by segmenting customers based on demographics, purchase history, and behavioural data. Automated email workflows, personalized messaging, and campaign analytics empower marketers to engage with customers at every stage of the buyer's journey.

4. **Workflow Management:** Each customer transaction goes from an initial sale to order fulfilment and can exist as both a simple "pick, pack & ship" or a more detailed and nuanced workflow with many decision points, customer interaction, 3rd party integrations and so forth.

5. **Customer Service and Support:** CRM facilitates seamless customer service by centralizing support tickets, inquiries, and feedback. Service teams can track issues, assign tasks, and resolve customer issues promptly, fostering satisfaction and loyalty.

Benefits of CRM for Businesses:

1. **Improved Customer Relationships:** By centralizing customer data and interactions, CRM enables businesses to better understand their customers' needs and preferences. This allows for more personalized communication and tailored offerings,

leading to stronger relationships and increased customer satisfaction.

2. **Consistent Business Processes:** A well structured CRM with integrated workflows means that each customer receives consistent messaging, handling and processing even if their individual order requirements are unique. Having all the information available to each stage of the order fulfilment process creates a single version of the truth for that client. No more hunting around for ad hoc scraps of paper, scribbled notes or misplaced emails.

3. **Enhanced Sales Performance:** CRM empowers sales teams with tools and insights to effectively manage leads, opportunities, and pipelines. By streamlining the sales process and providing real-time visibility into sales activities, CRM helps drive revenue growth and improve sales performance.

4. **Increased Efficiency and Productivity:** Automation features in CRM reduce manual tasks and streamline workflows across departments. This frees up time for employees to focus on high-value activities, such as building relationships, generating leads, and closing deals, thereby increasing overall efficiency and productivity.

5. **Data-Driven Decision Making:** CRM provides businesses with actionable insights and analytics to make informed decisions. By tracking key metrics such as sales performance, customer satisfaction, and marketing ROI, businesses can identify trends, optimize strategies, and drive continuous improvement.

6. **Scalability and Adaptability:** CRM solutions are scalable and adaptable to the evolving needs of businesses. Whether it's expanding customer base, launching new products, or entering new markets, CRM can flexibly accommodate growth and change, ensuring long-term success.

Different Types Of CRM

Selecting the appropriate Customer Relationship Management (CRM) software is a critical decision for any business aiming to optimize its operations and enhance customer relationships. With a plethora of options available in the market, understanding the different types of CRM software and their respective features is essential for making an informed choice.

Types of CRM Software

1. **Operational CRM**
   - Focuses on automating and streamlining front-office processes such as sales, marketing, and customer service.
   - Features include lead management, contact management, sales automation, marketing automation, and service ticketing.
   - Ideal for businesses looking to improve customer interactions and drive revenue growth through optimized sales and marketing efforts.

2. **Analytical CRM**
   - Emphasizes data analysis and insights generation to better understand customer behaviour and preferences.
   - Features include reporting, data mining, predictive analytics, and customer segmentation.
   - Suitable for businesses seeking to leverage data-driven decision-making and enhance

strategic planning and marketing effectiveness.

3. **Collaborative CRM**

    o Facilitates communication and collaboration across departments to ensure a unified approach to customer interactions.

    o Features include shared customer databases, communication tools, and workflow automation.

    o Beneficial for businesses with cross-functional teams that require seamless collaboration to deliver consistent and personalized customer experiences.

4. **Strategic CRM**

    o Aligns CRM initiatives with broader business objectives and long-term customer relationship goals.

    o Focuses on developing customer-centric strategies, loyalty programs, and customer lifetime value optimization.

- Suitable for businesses with a strategic focus on building long-term customer relationships and maximizing customer lifetime value.

Factors to Consider When Choosing CRM Software

1. **Business Needs and Objectives**

   - Assess your business requirements and objectives to determine the features and functionalities needed in a CRM solution.

   - Consider factors such as industry-specific requirements, organizational size, growth projections, and customer engagement goals.

2. **Scalability and Customization**

   - Choose a CRM solution that can scale with your business and accommodate future growth.

   - Look for customization options that allow you to tailor the software to meet your specific business processes and workflows.

3. **Integration Capabilities**

    o Ensure compatibility with existing systems and applications, such as ERP, marketing automation, and e-commerce platforms.

    o Select a CRM solution that offers seamless integration capabilities to avoid data silos and streamline operations.

4. **User Experience and Adoption**

    o Evaluate the user interface and usability of the CRM software to ensure ease of use and adoption by employees.

    o Look for intuitive features, mobile accessibility, and training resources to facilitate user adoption and maximize productivity.

5. **Data Security and Compliance**

    o Prioritize data security and compliance with industry regulations such as GDPR, HIPAA, or PCI-DSS.

- Choose a CRM solution with robust security features, data encryption, access controls, and compliance certifications.

6. **Vendor Reputation and Support**

    - Research the reputation and track record of CRM vendors in terms of product reliability, customer satisfaction, and support services.

    - Consider factors such as vendor stability, customer reviews, and availability of ongoing support and updates.

Selecting the right CRM software is a strategic decision that can significantly impact your business operations and customer relationships.

By understanding the different types of CRM software available and evaluating key factors such as business needs, scalability, integration capabilities, user experience, data security, and vendor reputation, businesses can make informed decisions and choose a CRM solution that aligns with their objectives and drives long-term success.

CHAPTER 4

Other Off-The-Shelf Solutions

While Customer Relationship Management (CRM) systems and (if you must) spreadsheets play crucial roles in managing customer relationships and data, businesses require a diverse array of software solutions to streamline various aspects of their operations.

From project management to accounting and inventory management, specialized software tools offer efficiency, automation, and optimization. In this chapter, we will provide an overview of some other popular software solutions beyond CRM and spreadsheets that businesses can leverage to streamline their operations effectively.

This chapter is not intended to be a full review of all other systems (or even a recommendation), but simply provides an insight into other systems and what they can do for a business.

Project Management Tools

1. **Trello**

    - Trello is a popular project management tool that utilizes boards, lists, and cards to organize tasks and workflows.

    - Features include task assignments, due dates, checklists, file attachments, and real-time collaboration.

    - Ideal for agile teams and collaborative projects, Trello promotes transparency, accountability, and productivity.

2. **Asana**

    - Asana is a versatile project management platform that enables teams to plan, track, and manage tasks and projects.

- Features include project timelines, task dependencies, Kanban boards, and workload management.

- With customizable workflows and integrations with other tools, Asana helps teams stay organized and focused on their goals.

3. **Jira**

    - Jira is a powerful project management and issue tracking software widely used in software development and IT teams.

    - Features include agile boards, scrum and Kanban methodologies, sprint planning, and bug tracking.

    - Designed for complex projects and teams, Jira offers advanced customization options and integration with development tools like Git and Confluence.

Accounting Software

1. **QuickBooks**

- QuickBooks is a leading accounting software solution for small and medium-sized businesses.

- Features include invoicing, expense tracking, payroll processing, financial reporting, and tax preparation.

- With cloud-based and desktop versions available, QuickBooks offers flexibility and scalability to meet the accounting needs of businesses across industries.

2. **Xero**

    - Xero is a cloud-based accounting software designed for small businesses and accountants.

    - Features include bank reconciliation, invoicing, inventory management, expense claims, and multi-currency support.

    - With real-time financial visibility and collaboration features, Xero helps businesses streamline accounting processes and make informed financial decisions.

3. **FreshBooks**

    o   FreshBooks is a user-friendly accounting and invoicing software tailored for freelancers and service-based businesses.

    o   Features include time tracking, project management, expense tracking, client portal, and payment processing.

    o   With intuitive interface and automation capabilities, FreshBooks simplifies invoicing and financial management for entrepreneurs and small teams.

Inventory Management Systems

1. **Fishbowl**

    o   Fishbowl is a robust inventory management solution designed for small and midsize businesses.

    o   Features include inventory tracking, order management, barcode scanning, asset management, and reporting.

- With integrations with QuickBooks and other accounting software, Fishbowl provides end-to-end visibility and control over inventory operations.

2. **TradeGecko**

    - TradeGecko is a cloud-based inventory management and order fulfilment platform for e-commerce businesses.

    - Features include inventory tracking, multi-channel sales management, automated reordering, and sales forecasting.

    - With real-time inventory syncing and centralized data management, TradeGecko helps businesses optimize inventory levels and streamline order fulfilment processes.

3. **NetSuite**

    - NetSuite is a comprehensive cloud-based ERP system that includes inventory management as part of its suite of business management solutions.

- Features include inventory control, demand planning, procurement, warehouse management, and supply chain visibility.

- With scalability and customization options, NetSuite caters to the inventory management needs of growing businesses across industries.

Benefits Of Integrating Off-The-Shelf Software Into Your Workflow

Whether it's integrating CRM, project management tools, accounting software, or inventory management systems, the seamless flow of data and processes across platforms can unlock numerous benefits for businesses.

Streamlined Processes and Data Flow

1. **Efficient Data Management**

    - Integration eliminates manual data entry and facilitates the seamless flow of information between systems.

- Data from CRM, project management, accounting, and inventory management systems can be synchronized in real-time, reducing errors and ensuring data accuracy.

2. **Automated Workflows**

    - Integrated systems enable the automation of repetitive tasks and workflows, saving time and improving efficiency.

    - For example, customer information captured in CRM can automatically populate invoices in accounting software, streamlining the invoicing process.

Enhanced Collaboration and Communication

1. **Cross-Functional Collaboration**

    - Integration fosters collaboration among teams by providing centralized access to information and streamlined communication channels.

    - Project teams can collaborate more effectively by accessing project-related data and updates from CRM, project management, and communication tools in one place.

2. **Improved Client Communication**

    o   Integrated systems enable better client communication and relationship management by providing a unified view of client interactions and history.

    o   Sales, marketing, and customer service teams can access client data and communication history from CRM and use it to personalize interactions and provide better service.

Data-Driven Decision Making

1. **Comprehensive Insights**

    o   Integrated systems provide comprehensive insights and analytics by combining data from multiple sources.

    o   Business leaders can gain a holistic view of operations, sales performance, financial health, and inventory levels, enabling informed decision-making and strategic planning.

2. **Predictive Analytics**

    o   Integrated systems leverage advanced analytics and predictive modelling to forecast trends, anticipate customer needs, and optimize resource allocation.

    o   For example, predictive analytics in CRM can help identify sales opportunities, while inventory management systems can forecast demand and optimize inventory levels accordingly.

Increased Efficiency and Productivity

1. **Reduced Duplication and Errors**

    o   Integration eliminates duplication of effort and reduces the risk of errors associated with manual data entry and inconsistent data across systems.

    o   Employees can focus on value-added tasks rather than spending time on data entry and reconciliation.

2. **Faster Response Times**

    o   Integrated systems enable faster response times to customer inquiries, orders, and requests by providing real-time access to relevant information.

    o   Sales, customer service, and fulfilment teams can respond promptly to customer needs, enhancing satisfaction and loyalty.

CHAPTER 5

Bespoke Software Solutions

While off-the-shelf software offers convenience and familiarity, bespoke software emerges as a compelling alternative for businesses seeking tailored solutions to meet their unique requirements.

Customization to Specific Business Needs

Off-the-shelf software solutions are designed to cater to a broad range of industries and use cases, often resulting in a one-size-fits-all approach. However, businesses operate in diverse environments with distinct processes and workflows.

Bespoke software allows businesses to tailor solutions precisely to their specific requirements, ensuring optimal functionality and performance. Whether it's automating complex business processes, integrating with existing systems, or implementing industry-specific features, bespoke software offers unparalleled customization capabilities.

Enhanced Functionality and Performance

Off-the-shelf software may offer a wide array of features, but businesses often find themselves compromising on functionality or performance to accommodate their unique needs. Bespoke software, on the other hand, enables businesses to prioritize critical functionalities and optimize performance according to their specifications.

By leveraging custom coding and architecture, bespoke solutions deliver enhanced functionality, reliability, and efficiency, thereby maximizing the value proposition for businesses.

Seamless Integration and Compatibility

Integrating off-the-shelf software with existing systems and infrastructure can pose significant challenges, leading to compatibility issues and data silos. Bespoke software solutions are built with integration in mind, allowing businesses to seamlessly connect with other systems and applications.

Whether it's integrating with legacy systems, third-party APIs, or cloud platforms, bespoke software ensures interoperability and data continuity across the entire business ecosystem.

Long-Term Cost-Efficiency and Return on Investment (ROI)

While off-the-shelf software may appear cost-effective initially, businesses often incur hidden costs associated with customization, licensing, and ongoing support.

Bespoke software solutions offer long-term cost-efficiency by eliminating unnecessary features and minimizing maintenance overhead. Moreover, bespoke software delivers a higher return on investment (ROI) by enhancing efficiency, productivity, and competitive advantage.

With tailored solutions designed to address specific business challenges, businesses can achieve tangible business outcomes and drive sustainable growth over time.

Scalability and Flexibility

As businesses evolve and grow, their software needs must adapt to changing requirements and scale accordingly.

Off-the-shelf software solutions may lack the flexibility to accommodate growth or necessitate costly upgrades and add-ons. Bespoke software solutions, however, are designed with scalability and flexibility in mind, allowing businesses to expand functionality, add new features, and support increased user volumes seamlessly.

Whether it's supporting new business processes, entering new markets, or accommodating regulatory changes, bespoke software empowers businesses to scale their operations efficiently.

Conclusion

While off-the-shelf software offers convenience and standardization, bespoke software emerges as the preferred choice for businesses seeking personalized, high-performance solutions. By prioritizing customization, functionality, integration, cost-efficiency, and scalability, businesses can leverage bespoke software to gain a competitive edge, drive innovation, and achieve their strategic objectives effectively.

Understanding The Risks Of Bespoke Software

Bespoke software certainly offers numerous advantages, such as customization and tailored functionality, but it also comes with its own set of risks and downsides.

Understanding these risks is crucial for businesses considering bespoke software development.

Some common risks of bespoke software and strategies for managing include:

Higher Initial Costs

- **Risk:** Bespoke software development often involves higher upfront costs compared to off-the-shelf solutions due to the custom development process.

- **Management:** Conduct a thorough cost-benefit analysis to evaluate the long-term value and return on investment (ROI) of bespoke software. Consider factors such as reduced operational costs, increased productivity, and competitive advantage over time.

Longer Development Time

- **Risk:** Developing bespoke software from scratch typically takes longer than implementing off-the-shelf solutions, potentially delaying the implementation timeline.

- **Management:** Work closely with the development team to establish realistic timelines and milestones. Prioritize features based on business needs and consider phased implementations to deliver key functionalities incrementally.

Uncertainty in Requirements

- **Risk:** Requirements for bespoke software may evolve over time, leading to scope creep, project delays, and budget overruns.

- **Management:** Conduct thorough requirements gathering and analysis upfront, involving stakeholders from across the organization. Implement change management processes to handle evolving requirements and prioritize flexibility in the software architecture to accommodate future changes.

Dependency on Development Partner

- **Risk:** Businesses may become dependent on the expertise of the development partner for ongoing support, maintenance, and updates.

- **Management:** Choose a reputable and experienced development partner with a proven track record of delivering successful bespoke software projects. Negotiate clear service-level agreements (SLAs) for ongoing support, maintenance, and upgrades. Consider establishing an internal team with knowledge of the software architecture to reduce dependency on external vendors.

Limited Third-Party Integration

1. **Risk:** Bespoke software may have limitations in integrating with third-party systems and applications, potentially leading to data silos and interoperability issues. This is particularly true of proprietary closed-loop software systems, but thankfully this is becoming less and less common.

2. **Management:** Prioritize interoperability and integration during the software design phase. Choose development frameworks and technologies that support standard protocols and APIs for seamless

integration with external systems. Conduct thorough testing to ensure compatibility and data consistency across integrated systems.

Maintenance and Updates

- **Risk:** Bespoke software requires ongoing maintenance, updates, and enhancements to address bugs, security vulnerabilities, and changing business requirements.

- **Management:** Establish a robust maintenance plan with regular updates and patches to address security vulnerabilities and ensure software stability. Invest in proper documentation and knowledge transfer to enable internal teams or future developers to maintain and enhance the software effectively. Consider implementing agile development practices to iterate and improve the software based on user feedback and evolving business needs.

Conclusion

While bespoke software offers numerous benefits, it also presents certain risks and challenges that businesses must be prepared to manage effectively. By proactively addressing risks related to cost, development time, requirements uncertainty, dependency on development partners, third-party integration, and maintenance, businesses can mitigate potential pitfalls and maximize the value of bespoke software solutions.

Through careful planning, collaboration, and ongoing management, businesses can leverage bespoke software to achieve their strategic objectives and drive long-term success.

CHAPTER 6

Working Out What Your Business Needs

Implementing a new software system is a significant undertaking for any organization, requiring careful planning, analysis, and execution. Conducting thorough business analysis is essential to ensure that the new system aligns with the organization's needs, objectives, and processes.

In this chapter, we will explore the key steps and best practices for conducting business analysis in readiness for implementing a new software system.

Define Objectives and Requirements

1. **Identify Business Objectives:** Start by defining the overarching business objectives and goals that the new software system should support. This could include improving operational efficiency, enhancing customer experience, or increasing revenue.

2. **Gather Stakeholder Requirements:** Engage stakeholders from across the organization to gather requirements and insights into their needs, pain points, and expectations from the new software system. Conduct interviews, workshops, surveys, and observation sessions to capture diverse perspectives.

3. **Prioritise Requirements:** Analyse and prioritize requirements based on their criticality, feasibility, and alignment with business objectives. Distinguish between must-have, should-have, and nice-to-have features to guide decision-making during the software selection process.

Assess Current Processes and Systems

1. **Document Existing Workflows:** Map out current business processes, workflows, and data flows to understand how the organization operates and where inefficiencies or bottlenecks exist.

2. **Identify Pain Points and Opportunities:** Identify pain points, gaps, and inefficiencies in current processes that the new software system should address. Look for opportunities to streamline operations, improve collaboration, and enhance decision-making.
3. **Evaluate Existing Systems:** Assess the strengths and weaknesses of existing systems and technologies to determine if they can be integrated with the new software system or if replacement is necessary.

Conduct Market Research

1. **Explore Available Solutions:** Research available software solutions in the market that align with the organization's requirements and objectives. Evaluate factors such as features, functionalities, scalability, vendor reputation, and total cost of ownership (TCO).

2. **Request Demos and Proposals:** Request demonstrations and proposals from software vendors to understand how their solutions address specific business needs and requirements. Ask questions, seek clarification, and gather information to make informed decisions.

3. **Consider Customization Options:** Assess the customization capabilities of software solutions to determine if they can be tailored to meet unique

business requirements without compromising functionality or scalability.

Develop Business Case and Implementation Plan

1. **Create a Business Case:** Develop a business case that outlines the rationale, benefits, and expected outcomes of implementing the new software system. Include cost estimates, ROI projections, and risk assessments to justify the investment to stakeholders.

2. **Define Implementation Plan:** Develop a detailed implementation plan that outlines the steps, timelines, resources, and responsibilities for deploying the new software system. Consider factors such as data migration, training, testing, and change management to ensure a smooth transition.

3. **Secure Executive Sponsorship:** Obtain executive sponsorship and support for the software implementation project to ensure buy-in from key stakeholders and allocate necessary resources.

Establish Success Metrics and Monitoring Mechanisms

1. **Define Key Performance Indicators (KPIs):** Establish measurable KPIs to track the success and impact of the new software system on business objectives. Examples include increased productivity, reduced turnaround time, and improved customer satisfaction.

2. **Implement Monitoring and Evaluation:** Set up mechanisms for monitoring and evaluating the performance of the new software system post-implementation. Gather feedback from users, analyze system usage data, and conduct periodic reviews to identify areas for improvement and optimization.

CHAPTER 7

Documenting Current/Desired Processes

This has briefly been covered in the previous chapter, but it is so fundamentally important, and crucially, is one of the major keys to success that it deserves further explanation.

It is often quoted that "a picture is worth a thousand words" and Art Degrees aside, pictures transform the clarity of the written word and avoids ambiguity.

Creating visual representations of business workflow processes is an invaluable practice that enhances understanding, communication, and analysis. In the following pages, we will explore the benefits of visualizing business workflow processes through diagrams and provide a step-by-step guide on how to create them effectively.

Benefits of Visualizing Business Workflow Processes

1. **Clarity and Understanding:** Visual diagrams provide a clear and intuitive representation of complex business processes, making it easier for stakeholders to grasp the sequence of activities, decision points, and dependencies.

2. **Communication and Collaboration:** Diagrams serve as a common language for communicating and collaborating with stakeholders across departments and organizational levels. They facilitate discussions, feedback, and consensus-building, leading to better alignment and shared understanding.

3. **Identifying Bottlenecks and Opportunities:** Visualizing workflow processes highlights bottlenecks, inefficiencies, and opportunities for improvement. By analysing the flow of activities and decision points, organizations can identify areas for optimization and innovation.

4. **Documentation and Knowledge Sharing:** Diagrams serve as valuable documentation of business processes,

capturing institutional knowledge and best practices. They provide a reference point for training, onboarding, and continuous improvement initiatives.

How-To Guide for Creating Business Workflow Diagrams

1. **Identify the Scope and Objective:** Define the scope of the workflow diagram and its intended purpose. Determine whether the focus is on a specific process, department, or cross-functional workflow.

2. **Gather Information and Stakeholder Input:** Engage stakeholders involved in the workflow to gather information about the sequence of activities, decision points, roles, and dependencies. Conduct interviews, workshops, or brainstorming sessions to ensure comprehensive input.

3. **Select the Right Diagramming Tool:** Choose a suitable diagramming tool based on the complexity of the workflow and the desired level of detail. Options include flowcharts, swimlane diagrams, process maps, and UML diagrams. Popular tools include Microsoft Visio, Lucidchart, and draw.io.

4. **Map Out the Workflow Steps:** Start by mapping out the high-level steps of the workflow using

standardized symbols and notation. Use shapes such as rectangles for activities, diamonds for decision points, and arrows for flow direction.

5. **Add Detail and Context:** Add additional detail to the diagram, including subprocesses, decision logic, inputs, outputs, and relevant documentation or references. Use annotations, labels, and colours to provide context and clarity.

6. **Create Wireframes:** A wireframe is little more than a hand-drawn screen layout and is a vital tool if you are looking to implement a bespoke solution or customise an off-the-shelf application. It shows the reader how you envisage the system actually looking albeit at a high level. Wireframes are linked to each other to show the reader how the process flow should fit from one stage to another. Software developers use wireframes extensively in their quest to truly understand the user requirements.

7. **Review and Iterate:** Review the draft diagram with stakeholders to validate accuracy, completeness, and clarity. Incorporate feedback and iterate on the diagram as needed to ensure alignment with business requirements and objectives.

8. **Finalize and Share:** Once the diagram is finalized, save it in a widely accessible format and share it with

relevant stakeholders. Consider embedding the diagram in documentation, presentations, or intranet portals for easy reference and access.

Conclusion

Visualizing business workflow processes through diagrams offers numerous benefits, including improved clarity, communication, analysis, and documentation. By following the step-by-step guide outlined in this chapter, organizations can create effective workflow diagrams that facilitate understanding, collaboration, and optimization of business processes. Through continuous refinement and sharing of workflow diagrams, organizations can drive operational excellence, innovation, and agility.

CHAPTER 8

Choosing The Right Vendor

By now, you will have a clear idea of what functionality you want the system (or systems) to deliver and how they should interoperate.

Define Requirements and Objectives

1. **Assess Business Needs:** Using the steps in the previous chapters, you'll have already conducted a thorough assessment of your organisation's requirements, challenges, and objectives. Identify the specific functionalities, features, and capabilities you

need from the software solution to support your digital transformation goals.

2. **Prioritise Requirements:** Prioritise your requirements based on their criticality and alignment with your strategic objectives. Distinguish between must-have, should-have, and nice-to-have features to guide vendor selection and contract negotiations. It is very easy to be wowed and get carried away with lots of shiny new toys, bells & whistles – and these can all be delivered – but focus on the essentials first.

Research and Shortlist Vendors

1. **Market Research:** Conduct market research to identify potential software vendors that offer solutions aligned with your requirements and objectives. Consider factors such as industry reputation, customer reviews, and market presence when shortlisting vendors.

2. **Ask Your Peers:** Most business owners or key decision makers know their industry peers and more often than not, most companies are not in a cut-and-thrust competitive industry. Simply talking with your peers

or members of relevant trade associations can provide valuable supplier information.

3. **Request Proposals:** Request proposals from shortlisted vendors, outlining your requirements, expectations, and evaluation criteria. Ask vendors to provide detailed information about their solutions, pricing models, implementation timelines, and support services.

Evaluate Vendor Capabilities

1. **Demo and Proof of Concept:** Schedule product demonstrations and request a proof of concept (POC) from vendors to assess the functionality, usability, and fit of their solutions. Involve key stakeholders from across the organization in the evaluation process to gather diverse perspectives.

2. **Reference Checks:** Reach out to existing customers and industry peers for references and testimonials about the vendor's performance, reliability, and customer support. Validate vendor claims and assess their track record of delivering successful implementations.

Negotiate Contract Terms

1. **Understand Pricing and Licensing:** Gain a clear understanding of the vendor's pricing models, licensing agreements, and fee structures. Negotiate pricing terms based on your budget constraints, scalability requirements, and expected ROI from the software solution.

2. **Customization and Support:** Negotiate terms related to customization, integration, and ongoing support services. Ensure that the contract includes provisions for addressing future updates, maintenance, and enhancements to the software solution.

3. **Data Security and Compliance:** Address data security and compliance requirements in the contract, including data ownership, privacy, and regulatory compliance. Ensure that the vendor adheres to industry standards and best practices for protecting sensitive information.

Establish Performance Metrics

1. **Service Level Agreements (SLAs):** Define clear service level agreements (SLAs) with the vendor to establish performance metrics, response times, and service guarantees. Specify penalties and remedies for

breaches of SLAs to ensure accountability and quality of service.

2. **Key Performance Indicators (KPIs):** Establish key performance indicators (KPIs) to measure the success and impact of the software solution on your business objectives. Monitor KPIs regularly and use them to track progress, identify areas for improvement, and drive continuous optimization.

Conclusion

Selecting the right software vendor and negotiating a favourable contract are critical steps in a company's digital transformation journey. By defining clear requirements, conducting thorough research, evaluating vendor capabilities, negotiating contract terms, and establishing performance metrics, companies can ensure they choose the best-fit vendor and secure a contract that aligns with their needs and objectives.

Through strategic vendor selection and contract negotiation, companies can lay the foundation for a successful digital transformation initiative that drives innovation, efficiency, and competitiveness in today's digital landscape.

CHAPTER 9

Managing The Project

Stereotypes exist for a reason and IT projects are notorious for being over budget, behind schedule and regularly lacking the desired functionality – somehow the final delivery bears as much resemblance to expectation as an architect's impression of a new-build housing estate, or the actual hamburger vs promised image of a Big Mac or Whopper.

It goes without saying that exceptional organisational skills and attention to detail are fundamental requirements for successfully managing a project and depending upon the type of system implementation your business is undertaking there are a number of different methodologies that can be employed.

Each methodology offers unique approaches to planning, executing, and delivering IT projects and below we will explore different types of IT project management methodologies, along with their respective pros and cons.

It is also worth noting that the project management methodology will most likely be determined by the various software vendors, especially in a bespoke development.

Types Of Project Management Methodologies

Waterfall Methodology

The waterfall methodology follows a linear, sequential approach, with each phase completed before moving to the next. Phases typically include requirements gathering, design, implementation, testing, deployment, and maintenance.

Pros:
- Clear project structure and predefined phases.
- Well-suited for projects with stable requirements and predictable outcomes.
- Easy to understand and manage progress.

Cons:
- Limited flexibility for changes once the project has started.

- Higher risk of scope creep and late-stage changes.
- Testing and validation occur late in the project lifecycle, potentially leading to costly rework.

Agile Methodology

Agile methodologies prioritize flexibility, collaboration, and iterative development. Agile frameworks, such as Scrum and Kanban, focus on delivering value incrementally through short iterations or sprints.

Pros:
- Adaptability to changing requirements and priorities.
- Continuous feedback loops promote stakeholder engagement and satisfaction.
- Early and frequent delivery of working software.

Cons:
- Requires active involvement and commitment from stakeholders.
- Initial learning curve for teams transitioning from traditional methodologies.
- Lack of upfront planning may lead to uncertainty in project scope and timelines.

Lean Methodology

Lean methodologies aim to eliminate waste and optimize efficiency by focusing on delivering value to the customer. Lean principles emphasize continuous improvement, workflow visualization, and minimizing work in progress (WIP).

Pros:
- Streamlined processes and reduced waste.
- Focus on customer value and satisfaction.
- Emphasis on collaboration and cross-functional teams.

Cons:
- May require cultural and organizational changes to embrace lean principles fully.
- Limited applicability to highly complex or long-term projects.
- Potential challenges in measuring and quantifying improvements in efficiency.

Scrum Framework

Scrum is an agile framework that emphasizes teamwork, collaboration, and iterative development. Scrum teams work in short, time-boxed iterations called sprints, typically lasting 2-4 weeks, to deliver working increments of the product.

Pros:

- Transparency and visibility into project progress through daily stand-up meetings, sprint reviews, and retrospectives.
- Empowerment of cross-functional, self-organizing teams.
- Flexibility to adapt to changing requirements and priorities.

Cons:

- Requires skilled Scrum Masters and Product Owners to facilitate and prioritize work effectively.
- May encounter challenges in scaling Scrum to larger teams or projects.
- Dependency on strong communication and collaboration among team members.

Kanban Methodology

Kanban is a lean methodology focused on visualizing workflow, limiting work in progress, and optimizing flow. Work items are represented as cards on a Kanban board, with columns representing different stages of the workflow.

Pros:

- Visual representation of work allows for easy tracking and identification of bottlenecks.
- Flexible and adaptable to different types of projects and workflows.

- Encourages continuous improvement through incremental changes.

Cons:
- Limited guidance on project planning and prioritization compared to other methodologies.
- Dependency on accurate metrics and data for effective workflow optimization.
- May require discipline to maintain WIP limits and avoid overloading the team.

The Project Manager Within Your Company

For a bespoke or heavily customised off-the-shelf solution your selected vendor(s) will most likely come with their own project manager. However, to ensure the smoothest and most successful implementation, your business will require an internal project manager to work hand-in-hand with the vendor's project manager.

When it comes to filling project manager roles, many companies overlook the potential of their existing staff pool and will seek a contract based project manager. However, promoting from within can offer numerous advantages, including insider knowledge, company culture alignment, and morale boost. In the section below, we'll explore the qualities that make a great project manager when hiring (or assigning) from within the existing company staff pool.

Deep Understanding of Company Culture and Processes

One of the key benefits of promoting from within is that internal candidates already have a deep understanding of the company's culture, values, and processes. They are familiar with the organization's goals, stakeholders, and operational dynamics, which allows them to hit the ground running and navigate challenges more effectively.

Knowledge of Company Systems and Tools

Internal candidates are likely to have experience working with the company's systems, tools, and processes. This familiarity enables them to leverage existing resources more efficiently, streamline workflows, and optimize project management practices. They can also provide valuable insights for improving or customizing existing tools to better suit project needs.

Established Relationships and Trust

Building strong relationships and trust is essential for effective project management. Internal candidates often have established relationships with key stakeholders, team members, and other departments within the organization. This existing rapport fosters collaboration, communication, and cooperation, leading to smoother project execution and better outcomes.

Institutional Knowledge and Historical Context

Internal candidates bring valuable institutional knowledge and historical context to their role as project manager. They understand the organization's history, previous projects, successes, failures, and lessons learned. This insight enables them to make more informed decisions, anticipate challenges, and apply past experiences to drive project success.

Alignment with Company Goals and Vision

Promoting from within ensures that project managers are aligned with the company's goals, vision, and strategic direction. Internal candidates are invested in the organization's success and have a vested interest in achieving positive outcomes for the company. Their commitment and dedication to the company's mission can inspire and motivate team members to excel.

Opportunity for Growth and Development

Offering career advancement opportunities to internal staff promotes employee engagement, loyalty, and retention. By investing in the development of existing talent, companies demonstrate their commitment to nurturing and empowering employees to reach their full potential. Providing training, mentorship, and support can help internal candidates transition into their new role as project managers successfully.

A Word Of Caution

For a project to be successful, it is paramount that the internal project manager is given time and space to work solely on the project. It is not a part-time task that can be casually assigned to the longest employed member of staff.

As your business invests in implementing new solutions, systems and processes it is foolish to do this without having a dedicated member of your staff fully engaged in the process.

CHAPTER 10

Implementing The New System

Transitioning to specialized software systems offers numerous benefits, including improved efficiency, accuracy, and scalability. However, making this transition requires careful planning and execution to ensure a smooth and successful implementation.

In this chapter, we will explore the key steps businesses can take to transition from spreadsheets to software solutions seamlessly. But first, let's recap the previous stages that have led us to this point.

The Journey So Far

Assess Current Processes and Requirements

Before embarking on the transition, businesses must conduct a comprehensive assessment of their current processes, workflows, and requirements. This includes:

- Identifying the functions and activities currently managed using spreadsheets.

- Evaluating the limitations and challenges associated with using spreadsheets, such as data silos, version control issues, and manual errors.

- Gathering requirements and feedback from stakeholders across departments to understand their needs and expectations from the new software solution.

Define Objectives and Success Criteria

Next, businesses should define clear objectives and success criteria for the transition. This involves:

- Establishing specific goals and objectives for implementing the new software solution, such as improving data accuracy, increasing productivity, or enhancing collaboration.

- Defining measurable key performance indicators (KPIs) to track the success and impact of the software implementation, such as reduced turnaround time, increased efficiency, and improved data quality.

Identify Suitable Software Solutions

Once requirements and objectives are defined, businesses can begin researching and evaluating suitable software solutions to replace spreadsheets. This includes:

- Exploring available software options in the market that align with business requirements and objectives.

- Requesting demos, trials, and consultations from software vendors to assess the functionality, usability, and suitability of their solutions.

- Considering factors such as scalability, integration capabilities, user experience, and total cost of ownership (TCO) when selecting a software solution.

Plan and Prepare for Implementation

Before implementing the new software solution, businesses should develop a comprehensive implementation plan and prepare accordingly. This involves:

- Creating a detailed project plan that outlines the steps, timelines, resources, and responsibilities for the implementation process.

- Identifying potential risks and challenges and developing mitigation strategies to address them proactively.

- Conducting training sessions and providing support to ensure that employees are prepared for the transition and familiar with the new software system.

Pilot Testing and Iterative Rollout

Rather than implementing the new software solution organization-wide at once, businesses can opt for a pilot testing approach followed by iterative rollout. This involves:

- Selecting a small group of users or departments to participate in the pilot testing phase.

- Gathering feedback and insights from pilot users to identify any issues, usability concerns, or areas for improvement.

- Iteratively rolling out the software solution to additional users or departments based on the feedback received during the pilot phase.

Monitor, Evaluate, and Optimize

Once the new software solution is implemented, businesses should continuously monitor, evaluate, and optimize its performance and usage. This includes:

- Tracking key performance indicators (KPIs) to assess the impact of the software solution on business objectives and outcomes.

- Gathering feedback from users and stakeholders to identify areas for improvement and optimization.

- Iteratively refining and enhancing the software solution based on user feedback and changing business requirements.

Strategies for Employee Training and Adoption of New Systems

On the whole, people don't like change and transitioning to new software systems requires more than just technological implementation; it involves ensuring that employees are adequately trained and motivated to adopt and use the new systems effectively.

Tailored Training Programs

1. **Assess Training Needs:** Conduct a thorough assessment of employees' existing skills, knowledge, and proficiency levels related to the new software system. Identify areas where additional training or support may be required.

2. **Customize Training Programs:** Develop tailored training programs based on employees' roles, responsibilities, and learning preferences. Offer a mix of online tutorials, classroom sessions, hands-on workshops, and one-on-one coaching to accommodate diverse learning styles.

3. **Provide Continuous Support:** Offer ongoing training and support resources to employees even after the initial rollout. Provide access to training materials, user guides, FAQs, and helpdesk support to address questions and challenges as they arise.

Hands-On Learning and Practice

1. **Interactive Workshops:** Organize interactive workshops and simulation exercises where employees can practice using the new software system in a controlled environment. Encourage hands-on learning and experimentation to build confidence and proficiency.

2. **Role-Based Scenarios:** Develop role-based scenarios and case studies that simulate real-world situations and challenges encountered in employees' daily tasks. Allow employees to apply their learning to practical scenarios relevant to their roles.

3. **Peer Learning and Mentoring:** Foster a culture of peer learning and mentoring where experienced users can share their knowledge and best practices with newer or less experienced colleagues. Encourage collaboration and knowledge sharing among employees to accelerate learning and adoption.

Clear Communication and Expectations

1. **Communicate Benefits and Purpose:** Clearly communicate the benefits and purpose of the new software system to employees, emphasizing how it will improve efficiency, streamline processes, and support their work objectives.

2. **Set Expectations:** Set clear expectations regarding the transition timeline, training requirements, and performance goals related to the adoption of the new system. Define success criteria and milestones to track progress and celebrate achievements.

3. **Address Resistance and Concerns:** Proactively address any resistance or concerns among employees regarding the transition to the new system. Listen to their feedback, address their concerns, and involve them in decision-making processes to increase buy-in and ownership.

Continuous Feedback and Improvement

1. **Gather User Feedback:** Solicit feedback from employees throughout the transition process to identify areas for improvement and optimization. Use surveys, focus groups, and feedback mechanisms to gather insights into user experiences and challenges.

2. **Iterative Training Approach:** Adopt an iterative approach to training and adoption, refining and enhancing training programs based on user feedback and evolving business needs. Continuously update training materials and resources to address emerging requirements and challenges.

3. **Celebrate Successes:** Recognize and celebrate successes and achievements related to the adoption of the new software system. Highlight examples of successful implementation and user stories to inspire and motivate employees to embrace the change.

Conclusion

Effective employee training and adoption strategies are critical for the successful implementation of new software systems. By tailoring training programs to employees' needs, providing hands-on learning opportunities, communicating clear expectations, and soliciting continuous feedback, businesses can foster a culture of learning, collaboration, and innovation. Through proactive support, engagement, and recognition, businesses can empower employees to embrace change, maximize the value of new systems, and drive organizational success.

CHAPTER 11

Overcoming Resistance To Change

As you embark on this process, your business will meet resistance – either passively or, depending upon company culture, quite aggressively.

People don't tend to like change – it creates a sense of fear and uncertainty and there will inevitably be the nay-sayers. Below is a list of common objections and ideas to how they can be addressed in a positive manner.

Cost Concerns

Objection: "The new software solution is too expensive, and we're unsure about the return on investment (ROI)."

Addressing Strategy

- Conduct a thorough cost-benefit analysis to quantify the potential savings and benefits of the new software solution.

- Highlight long-term cost savings, increased efficiency, and competitive advantages gained from the new system.

- Offer flexible payment options, such as monthly subscriptions or phased implementations, to ease financial concerns.

Resistance to Change

Objection: "We're comfortable with our current processes and hesitant to change."

Addressing Strategy

- Emphasize the benefits of the new software solution, such as improved productivity, streamlined workflows, and enhanced capabilities.

- Provide training and support to help employees adapt to the new system and alleviate fears of the unknown.

- Involve employees in the decision-making process and communicate the reasons behind the change to gain buy-in and ownership.

Integration Challenges

Objection: "We're concerned about integrating the new software solution with our existing systems and processes."

Addressing Strategy

- Conduct a comprehensive compatibility assessment to identify potential integration challenges and solutions proactively.

- Work closely with the software vendor to develop a customized integration plan and roadmap.

- Invest in middleware or integration tools to facilitate data exchange and interoperability between systems.

Data Security and Privacy

Objection: "We're worried about data security and privacy risks associated with the new software solution."

Addressing Strategy

- Select a reputable software vendor with a proven track record of prioritizing data security and compliance.

- Review the software vendor's security measures, certifications, and compliance with industry standards (e.g., GDPR, HIPAA).

- Implement robust security protocols, encryption mechanisms, and access controls to safeguard sensitive data and mitigate risks.

Lack of Customization

Objection: "The new software solution doesn't meet our specific requirements and needs."

Addressing Strategy

- Collaborate with the software vendor to customize and tailor the solution to align with your organization's unique requirements.

- Identify key customization options and features that can address specific pain points or workflow challenges.

- Prioritize flexibility and scalability in the software architecture to accommodate future customization and enhancements.

Implementation Complexity

Objection: "We're concerned about the complexity and disruption associated with implementing the new software solution."

Addressing Strategy

- Develop a comprehensive implementation plan with clear milestones, timelines, and responsibilities.

- Assign dedicated project teams and resources to oversee the implementation process and address any challenges promptly.

- Provide training, support, and resources to help employees navigate the transition and minimize disruption to daily operations.

Performance and Reliability

Objection: "We're unsure about the performance and reliability of the new software solution."

Addressing Strategy

- Conduct thorough testing and evaluation of the software solution to ensure reliability, scalability, and performance under different scenarios.

- Seek references and testimonials from existing customers or industry peers to validate the vendor's claims and track record.

- Implement contingency plans and backup procedures to mitigate risks and minimize downtime in case of system failures or disruptions.

Strategies For Overcoming Employee Resistance

Communicate the Why & Explain The Reasons

Clearly communicate the reasons behind the change, emphasizing the benefits and opportunities it will bring to both the organization and individual employees. Help them understand the purpose and significance of the new system in achieving business goals.

Address Concerns

Encourage open dialogue and address employees' concerns and apprehensions about the change. Listen to their feedback, validate their concerns, and provide transparent and honest responses to build trust and credibility.

Involve Employees & Engage Stakeholders

Involve employees in the decision-making process from the early stages of planning and implementation. Solicit their input, feedback, and suggestions to ensure that their needs and perspectives are considered in the design and rollout of the new system.

Create Champions

Identify influential employees or "change champions" who can advocate for the new system and help drive adoption among their peers. Empower these champions with training, resources, and support to lead by example and inspire others to embrace the change.

Provide Training and Support

Provide comprehensive training and support to help employees learn how to use the new system effectively. Offer various training formats, such as workshops, tutorials, videos, and hands-on sessions, to accommodate different learning styles and preferences.

Tailor Training to Roles

Customize training programs to align with employees' roles, responsibilities, and skill levels. Focus on practical, job-relevant training that demonstrates how the new system will improve their workflows, productivity, and job satisfaction.

Highlight Success Stories – Share Early Wins

Celebrate early successes and achievements resulting from the new system implementation. Share success stories, case studies, and testimonials from early adopters to showcase the positive impact of the change and inspire others to follow suit.

Recognize and Reward

Recognize and reward employees who embrace the change, demonstrate proficiency with the new system, and contribute to its successful adoption. Use incentives, rewards, and acknowledgment to reinforce desired behaviours and motivate continued engagement.

Foster a Supportive Culture - Promote Collaboration

Foster a culture of collaboration, teamwork, and knowledge sharing that encourages employees to support and help each other during the transition. Facilitate cross-departmental collaboration and peer-to-peer learning to build a sense of community and shared ownership.

Encourage Feedback

Create channels for employees to provide feedback, suggestions, and ideas for improvement throughout the change process. Actively listen to their feedback, implement changes based on their input, and demonstrate a commitment to continuous improvement.

Monitor Progress and Adjust

Establish key performance indicators (KPIs) to measure the adoption and utilization of the new system over time. Monitor adoption metrics, user feedback, and support tickets to identify areas of success and areas for improvement.

Iterate and Improve

Use feedback and performance data to iteratively refine and improve the new system and its implementation strategy. Be flexible and willing to make adjustments as needed to address evolving needs, challenges, and opportunities.

CHAPTER 13

Maximizing The Benefits

Once the s software solutions have been implemented, it is really down to the business to make sure that all opportunities and benefits are maximised.

This is not a "one and done" type process – your business is a living, breathing entity and so are the systems and processes that you have implemented.

Maximizing the benefits of software solutions, including data analysis and automation, requires a comprehensive approach that leverages technology to its fullest potential. Below are some key strategies to help business optimise the value derived from the systems that have been implemented.

Define Clear Objectives and Key Performance Indicators (KPIs)

Clearly define the objectives and desired outcomes that the software solution is intended to achieve. Ensure that these objectives are aligned with the organization's overarching business goals and strategic priorities.

Establish KPIs

Identify key performance indicators (KPIs) that will be used to measure the success and impact of the software solution. These KPIs should be specific, measurable, achievable, relevant, and time-bound (SMART), providing quantifiable metrics for evaluating performance and ROI.

Data-driven Decision Making

Leverage the capabilities of the software solution to collect, analyze, and visualize data from various sources within the organization. Use advanced analytics techniques, such as predictive modeling, machine learning, and data mining, to gain actionable insights and identify trends, patterns, and opportunities for optimization.

Real-time Monitoring

Implement real-time monitoring and reporting capabilities to track key metrics and performance indicators dynamically. Use dashboards, reports, and alerts to provide stakeholders with timely and accurate information for making informed decisions and taking proactive actions.

Process Optimization and Automation

Conduct process mapping and analysis to identify bottlenecks, inefficiencies, and areas for improvement within existing workflows. Use the software solution to streamline processes, eliminate unnecessary steps, and optimize resource allocation to improve efficiency and productivity.

Automation

Leverage automation capabilities offered by the software solution to automate repetitive tasks, manual processes, and routine workflows. Automate data entry, document generation, approval workflows, and other routine activities to reduce human error, save time, and free up resources for higher-value tasks.

Integration and Collaboration

Integrate the software solution with other systems and tools used across the organization to ensure seamless data exchange and interoperability. Integrate with ERP systems, CRM platforms, HRIS, and other business applications to create a unified data ecosystem and streamline information flow.

Promote Collaboration

Use the software solution to facilitate collaboration and communication among team members, departments, and stakeholders. Implement features such as document sharing, task assignment, and project management tools to foster collaboration, transparency, and accountability.

Continuous Improvement

Adopt an iterative approach to software optimization and improvement, continuously monitoring performance, gathering feedback, and making incremental enhancements based on user input and evolving business needs.

Training and Development

Provide ongoing training and support to employees to ensure they have the skills and knowledge needed to leverage the full potential of the software solution. Offer regular training sessions, workshops, and resources to keep users up-to-date with new features, best practices, and industry trends.

Conclusion

By implementing these strategies, organizations can maximize the benefits of software solutions, including data analysis and automation, to drive business growth, innovation, and competitive advantage.

By aligning software initiatives with business objectives, harnessing the power of data-driven insights, optimizing processes through automation, fostering collaboration, and embracing a culture of continuous improvement, organizations can unlock the full potential of their software investments and achieve sustainable success.

CHAPTER 14

Looking Ahead

Having invested in your business and leveraged the most that software systems can currently offer, it is important not to sit back and simply think "job done".

To get this far has taken a herculean effort and technology is an ever changing beast. Staying ahead of the curve is essential for businesses to remain competitive and relevant.

As technology continues to advance, new trends in software development are emerging, reshaping the way organizations operate and interact with their customers.

In the following paragraphs, we'll explore future (and current) trends in software development and strategies for leveraging them to continuously improve business processes and drive success.

Trends in Software Development

Artificial Intelligence (AI) and Machine Learning

AI and machine learning are revolutionizing software development by enabling systems to learn from data, adapt to new information, and make intelligent decisions autonomously. From predictive analytics to natural language processing, AI-powered solutions are enhancing efficiency, personalization, and automation across various industries.

Internet of Things (IoT)

The Internet of Things (IoT) is connecting devices, sensors, and objects to the internet, enabling seamless communication and data exchange. IoT-powered solutions offer real-time insights, remote monitoring, and automation capabilities, transforming industries such as manufacturing, healthcare, and logistics.

Edge Computing

Edge computing involves processing data closer to its source, reducing latency and improving performance for mission-critical applications. With the proliferation of IoT devices and the need for real-time processing, edge computing is becoming increasingly important for businesses seeking to leverage data-driven insights and optimize operations.

Blockchain Technology

Blockchain technology offers secure, transparent, and decentralized data storage and transactions, eliminating the need for intermediaries and enhancing trust and security. From supply chain management to financial transactions, blockchain-powered solutions are revolutionizing processes and enabling new business models.

Low-Code/No-Code Development

Low-code and no-code development platforms empower business users to create custom applications and automate workflows without extensive coding knowledge. These platforms accelerate development cycles, enable rapid prototyping, and promote collaboration between business and IT teams.

Strategies for Continuous Improvement through Technology Adoption

Stay Informed and Educated

Keep abreast of emerging technologies, industry trends, and best practices through continuous learning, attending conferences, and networking with peers. Invest in training and development programs to upskill employees and empower them to leverage new technologies effectively.

Foster a Culture of Innovation

Create an environment that encourages experimentation, creativity, and risk-taking. Empower employees to explore new ideas, pilot projects, and implement innovative solutions that drive business value and competitive advantage.

Embrace Agile and DevOps Practices

Adopt agile and DevOps methodologies to streamline development processes, accelerate time-to-market, and improve collaboration between development, operations, and business teams. Embrace automation, continuous integration, and continuous delivery (CI/CD) practices to ensure rapid and reliable software delivery.

Focus on Customer Experience

Prioritize customer-centricity and user experience in software development efforts. Solicit feedback from customers, gather user insights, and iterate on product designs to ensure that software solutions meet customer needs and expectations.

Collaborate with Technology Partners

Forge strategic partnerships with technology vendors, startups, and industry experts to gain access to cutting-edge solutions, expertise, and resources. Collaborate with external partners to co-innovate, share knowledge, and stay at the forefront of technological advancements.

Invest in Scalable and Flexible Solutions

Select software solutions that are scalable, flexible, and future-proof to accommodate evolving business needs and technology trends. Leverage cloud-based platforms, microservices architecture, and modular design principles to build agile and adaptable systems that can scale with your business.

Conclusion

No-one has a working crystal ball and as businesses navigate an increasingly complex and dynamic digital landscape, embracing future trends in software development is crucial for driving innovation, enhancing efficiency, and staying ahead of the competition.

By prudently leveraging technologies such as AI, IoT, edge computing, blockchain, and low-code development, organizations can unlock new opportunities, optimize processes, and deliver value to customers.

By adopting a strategic approach to technology adoption, fostering a culture of innovation, and embracing agile practices, businesses can continuously improve business processes and position themselves for long-term success.

CHAPTER 15

Final Thoughts

Spreadsheets are incredible tools and have come a long way since VisiCalc and Lotus 1-2-3 back in the 80's, but their flexibility and ease-of-use has led many businesses of all shapes and sizes to allow this tool to become fundamental to the day to day operating of their business.

Depending upon which bit of research you read, anywhere up to 81% of business use spreadsheets. And that's great – it means a global talent pool can use what is an undeniably useful tool.

But what rapidly evolves is that a "quick & dirty spreadsheet list" becomes an instrumental document for business processes - and that is just plain dangerous.

In 2016 I was asked to work with a contract flooring company to review their back office processing. The Managing Director noticed that his 20+ staff were calling out to each other saying "can someone shut down XYZ spreadsheet as I need to update the customer information" on an almost continuous basis.

Worse still, in this particular company there was a gentleman called Billy who was using an almost incomprehensible and glaringly fluorescently colour-coded spreadsheet to manage all of the site installations. Without a word of a lie, whenever Billy took a day off or went on annual leave, other staff would rush to book the same time off or actually call in sick because, in their words, "no-one wants Billy's job".

Even with an impressive client list (including many globally recognised household names and brands), and a turnover of several million pounds a year, this company still relied upon a number of garishly coloured spreadsheets to manage their entire operation.

Another client of mine, who had a client list of over 100,000 individuals was managing their clients trust funds and investments (worth hundreds of millions) using a publicly accessible Google Sheet.

And so the list goes on.

But in every case, the business owners were not fools. They had all built successful businesses, servicing clients all over the world, but they had let their businesses become totally and utterly dependent upon the world's largest bit of graph paper.

These things just creep up on you and in many cases, the old adage of "if it ain't broke, don't fix it" can ring true – but, if you want to scale your business, or maximise all the benefits that technology has to offer, then you need to be looking beyond the spreadsheet.

It is my fervent hope that, if you've got this far, you can see the huge potential of leveraging software solutions for growth and efficiency – and it would be my absolute pleasure to work with you and your business on this journey.

If you would like to reach out, then feel free to email me at

dan@a2solutions.co.uk

ABOUT THE AUTHOR

Since getting my first computer, a Sinclair ZX Spectrum, back in 1982, I knew that I wanted to spend the rest of my life building software solutions for businesses. A 16 year corporate career in finance provided an education and exposure to many types of businesses and in 2004, I left the corporate world to start my own software company and fulfil my childhood ambition.

While I don't have much of an ego, I genuinely do get a huge sense of achievement knowing that, in this world, there are systems that I (along with my amazingly talented team) have designed and built that not only enable businesses to perform as optimally as possible (or even exist) but that there are people, actual human beings, who continue to benefit from these systems on a daily basis.

www.ingramcontent.com/pod-product-compliance
Lightning Source LLC
Chambersburg PA
CBHW050112230526
45470CB00004B/1794